Testimonials

In this collection of sonnet-like meditations, Noel Jeffs achieves a joyful tone of curious inquisition and wonder. Rich in literary allusion and mindful self-reflection these poems make a fine dwelling at the start of each day.

Phillip Hall
Fume UWAP, Borroloola Class IPSI & Cactus Recent Work Press

Walking in Stealth uses the author's love of words — and of playing with words — as a vehicle with which to explore his 'own coastline' — sometimes through difficult terrain ('Tonight will I be chased through the mirrors again?'), and sometimes towards moments of grace, but always with an eye on what it means to be oneself: as Jeffs says, in the closing lines — "Touching my own solace in a country of queer and light. Touching my own substance of aliveness beyond claim."

Martin Langford

This is a work sown with ambition and harvested with rhyme and a formal and reverential diction. The minimal punctuation makes demands on the reader but conveys a unity suggestive of the epic, albeit personally-dimensioned in this case. Meditation, prayer, lament, a paean to friendship, topical awareness, his past, the everyday traffic of life — all find their way into Jeffs' journey of the self which, since this **is** poetry, glories in the word, as it must.

Paul Scully
Decision Horizons

At first it seems like rushing, then slow motion, baby steps one moment, giant strides another. So many combinations, dimensions, fusions-oppositions and lots between. Sensation, emotion, thought, spirit poured into fleeting images, word play and soul play. Glancing blows, deep wounds — and when you re-read and re-read again — worlds within worlds, places we live, an inpouring-outpouring of life.

Michael Eigen, PhD
The Challenge of Being Human, Faith, The Sensitive Self

Over the six decades I have known Noel Jeffs, I have known a person who has a strong social conscience and a deep concern and passion for a wide range of societal issues. With the Russian poet, playwright and novelist, Pushkin, as one of his mentors Noel Jeffs has addressed a diverse range of social issues in this anthology.

I commend this publication to you as it is a timeless resource that will continue to enrich and bless people well into the future.

God bless

Bill Ray

Walking in Stealth

After Pushkin

This is an IndieMosh book

brought to you by MoshPit Publishing
an imprint of Mosher's Business Support Pty Ltd

PO Box 4363
Penrith NSW 2750

indiemosh.com.au

 A catalogue record for this work is available from the National Library of Australia

https://www.nla.gov.au/collections

Title:	Walking in Stealth
Subtitle:	After Pushkin
Author:	Jeffs, Noel (SSF)
ISBNs:	9781922912091 (paperback) 9781922912107 (ebook – epub) 9781922912114 (ebook – Kindle)
Subjects:	POETRY / Australian & Oceanian; Subjects & Themes / Inspirational & Religious

No individual in these poems is taken from real life. Any resemblance to any person or persons living or dead is accidental and unintentional. The author, their agents and publishers cannot be held responsible for any claim otherwise and take no responsibility for any such coincidence.

Cover concept by Noel Jeffs SSF.

Cover design and layout by Sarah Davies at www.instagram.com/lemon.design.studios.

Cover image of Magpie from Adobe Stock.

Walking in Stealth

After Pushkin

Noel Jeffs SSF

Also by Noel Jeffs SSF:

Maturing in the Religious Life

*This is a series of meditations written in the morning light
with culture in mind.*

*They were my morning meditations as the sun rose
over my right shoulder and dawned the day with sunlight
at the break of day.*

Written as a series of poems after Pushkin, as a thesis for the Masters of
Creative Writing (granted) at Sydney University 2017

Contents

They parade their stealth, have no wealth

They rolled with their oars

Plundered with the waves

Until the lisp had its shores

Were caught in as greaves?

I had been suffocated was

Design as its crush a pizazz

Designed is to be for inlaid

Cursory language as blade

As stroll tidy as hemstitched

Harvested so long as a bed

Dipped mine rolled sass red

I sailed along as feed a long

To avoid the wounds of song

Noel Jeffs

How they shadow you and plunder you

How they shadow you as for an engrossed

To plunder you as tame and just for a fare

For the stroking of the mane of their post

Yet I find in the tallow wood a new heart

It rigours fine wood, and it colours yellow

Beyond the stroking of knees, and its tides

The wisdom of not taking their fabled rides

Lost bites, anew as meridians are for loess

Gog and Magog would temper words gloss

Am I lost in a wildness of this morning's toil?

I crest my own waves, a creole of land rights

For days are not yet indicting of black nights

My shopping window today

I wear a pigtail and have learnt to trust its open gold

I don't wear a pinafore, or a pine plantation of panic

I creep through indents of day, envy cannot be sold

If queer country could always be and was as a tonic

To cross its rivers and mountains, open or deigned

Where there is no crepe from a world of arraigned

Where there is no Cythera as life-lines so barbarous

Refused a countersink of sound, mania as murderous

I am ground to my own grist, a toil muscular and plain

To cafe with the washings of others lusting grossness

To open my own heart into solace as a wit's fastness

To grope through luminous words a pander to claim

Settle myself again a Cumberland's stone of lushness

Open windows words to refuse hemstitch's plushness

Noel Jeffs

Past repression; a repair

Is it sunshine in light to have stood a ground

Refusing the whips of trade cutlets for minds

The sow of the morning is a silence of sound

The awakening of the opening light in grains

Holding its reigning, making grates of skyline

As plenitude might fly with coat pegs of time

Beyond a grumbling a quaking of words plain

Stretching the palms for the truth of its seine

Finds the opening of this day a deafly stillness

And made a portal in its semblance of a heart

Beyond striking pivotal drunkenness of a girth

As if the songlines for this day rankling fullness

To pull past the sirens of driveness and a pain

Toss my grumbling leg and walk without feign

Land mark

We were still last night in musing through a world of chattering

In a land designed as banquet, and made our own supposition

A deceptive model, but strung well as for of town its gathering

Designed invocation of a beer's corona drunk wine's apposition

Cruelled the borders miraculously and minuscule was its dregs

Captured word and vein as bird's silence made against the kegs

This holding our own cravenness it's loving as made is openness

Receptiveness of turning water into a wine is beyond a sowing

The banqueting hall as made a freshness and in its own fidelity

Beyond the space of words, or finding grace as making all quake

A fixity to be held was in the occasion of its loan made forcraic

Trust a day of lack trust a day of mains for even holding its vanity

Trust the construing of heart in another city place as its own grace

Opened as the last vast syllable of my unstressed and loving face

Stillness is a unique preposition

We were still last night in a chattering-box world

In a design land of banquet made as supposition

A deceptive world made of beer, as I chose wine

Crossed those borders miraculously of opposition

Brought life's dilemmas, a being alone in aliveness

Captured words vein, to touch spaces cravenness

Though as sideline and with a loving of openness

Made small realm's friendship wade as freshness

The banqueting hall trimmed as a lore of liturgy

Speels Vietnamese a flurry of gin and a creativity

Sauntered a nights shadowing. Other embolding

Through landmark of gathering timed delightfully

The open spaces of a day, made its tea ceremony

And the search as that unstressed die of a loving

Unrestricted for alliance with poetry

A world of dancing demands open spaces of a realm

Beyond another's world has plain sailing into nuance

To dream big into the horizons of finding this gleam

Infinities dreaming as capturing serving its dalliance

To find beyond groove, greaves made of two-pence

Lasting through spaces of hunger, as a world's fence

Opening horizons clamour is given as to their others

Emboldening dimensions of landscape are heirlooms

Not first born, born to the rigours for its aloneness's

Dreaming through graces given as has for its tailings

Finding the mining, being water wheels of its railings

Holds a dimension of gathering broom flower estate

Holding, spacing, treading in groove of a classic taste

It becomes a burden, but a loving challenge, of chaste

We were a small wee of the morning dispensing the unity of food

We were a desiccated heart opening its mind to sowing aliveness

And beginning again as serial run in search of another good mood

Opening to pages beyond words in the taming, as made tribeness

To tarry too long within was a strange lands gaming apprehension

Still collecting a dust for we're its mementos and a roar of ghosts

Still, as scarpered body through these pages as made for moating

Beyond a world of gloating, just astringent was for all a goathing

As I collected like a seance or made as in the visits of these spirits

Without the shrew, and a piddling of the day just open to ensue

Opening my heart, resisting my back to walk like a times parvenu

Not driven but catching it was as for words and as making tryffids

A searching for this sailing ship is to catch as wind hover of places

And avoiding the roiling of Larry do, traffics mores have as traces

A turpentine forest

It's pale and glowing when morning casting sows its shadow

Twisting through the palings of its fences into a risible gold

Touched my windows, as overlocking with the railway lines

To bring past these dooms of a paradise's sustenance hold

Where cant is refused and songs are continued as boldness

An interlocking demon without the vengeance of a roilness

Grooming has made a new life for wearing its own talisman

Past aspirations are renewed now played into as perchance

Past a Cistercian hold on life nor even as a Clairvaux's crafts

Gathering sound waves, an openness crafts within a silence

Not trivialized, gathering both darkness and highs pretense

Not mirroring but as flowing into now has a face of my own

Flooring is colour, with all its drams of an aspiration's desire

Flavouring beyond Technicolor to find this hue's a pallid lyre

Refusing to be windsurfed, I am my own coastline-recovery of my sotto voice-I am made complete in poetry

I saw their painting as a daguerreotype, and I prefer sounds

I refuse to be taken to shore with its sun surfing in my wings

And in the winds of the morning I found my love of grounds

Driveness doesn't bring beyond to my sands but just things

Completeness is a maiden's desire to open a heart line again

To rustle the quietness in a new day gathering for this seine

Opening up the derivatives discovering where a rain is falling

To avoid the plundering by hearts made through their railing

And breaking through disparate nights made of lost children

Widening into distinction between its lower and north shore

To hold my heart within its place has the wisdom of its flora

Crying of their blackness ladles its silk silently to my rendition

Avoiding in the lasting ghosts of its treadled machine's wheel

The strength of opening up my day as made its own greeting

My own fire of landing. Lament

Tonight will I be chased through the mirrors again?

Will I be treated an oblate of kind, even as though

I foresee 1 chase others into their mirroring of time

Remembering they come in withers, healing a blow

Invade space trample break through take my mind

The sentient passed, wounding to feed was to heal

I refuse to be a captive race sundered by this place

Cried to my own tribe, as given as gizzards of grace

I pass for dregs of sorrow reframe its righteousness

So broken into so broken, as I was beached in push

The word of refusing as scarpering is my own truck

A loaded back or a writing space as my creativeness

I sense in time I have been plundered before wailing

No other things as a timeless land longing for a sand

A breakfast time and lightened world where openness imagines

The gathering of space and horizons fade as words are costume

Beyond a devilish trial of not receding made for was face's train

Just hoping all this made time that as its well-constructed loom

Beyond hopping lamely, and a creating moon where words sing

Beyond intransigence looms don't fade where I find voices ping

Trialing one moment after the other as dervish's for a moment

Walking through the painfulness of existence in a plain torment

Silently captivated by endurances holding of its own bold claim

Holding spleen for a craic that is awakeness made for morning

Soldering agency as its claim for a polemic again as a swooning

A livening gleam in my eye, as made from the duress of eglaim

This holding to worth for, is like my holding to north for its gay

A chrism as of its bain, a baking, solidly as for a walking of dray

In house Parousia: refusing to be repressed

It was a blizzard that tried to take hold

The same way that a white-out spooks

Its rue seemed to grow as it seeded sold

I am not derivative that I can't see a Luke

I didn't let it grow as like a corner stone

Fed wiles to let it hang through my bone

Walked pasture as clement to gathering

If l could pantoum try perfume lathering

I have need of my own words for release

For as the arch-lode that is an after-mind

Is not to be fused, as ladling for its drains

Avoid graze for simplicity is made a piece

In the ease of refusing was to be as soak

Captivities splendid turning as new drake

Noel Jeffs

In the division of time much is spent in array

I cloak the mien of garthing the loads of crie

Without a derision I discover how lords play

Holding my own reigns for its parade as lye

Facing passages of a locked key and a storm

Dreamt my own dreaming again to relearn

Finding me a grue that takes as spent couth

In the morning light as a muse hungry ruth

Under a crimson skyline clouds are growth

After speechlessness had signed it's driven

My tongue had foregone words as toward

Seeking a life pastured as passion, drought

Until I crossed words, a wold of its gravure

Making as semblance for this non-sequitur.

Through the strength of daylight

I felt as though consumed, and in my bed rolled

And I cast my bread upon the waters of writing

As though in an early dawning something tolled

Like in a cucumber desiring oppressed for lilting

I touched my own lips, as had its sore heads tile

Until I saw my day was not to riddle or for a soil

And in the opening of a light shining for a glow

I pursed in words making as the voice of its soul

A desire to silence could plug into rhythms goal

Over-flying, as a spandrel of a chuffing its crow

Harking to its life again is making a meal's hope

Here workmen are toiling through a life's shape

– For literature and life – in a morning's lauds –

The daylight is shrew

I am turned to light as opening the eyes of darkness

Beyond a ravens thorp, a ravens hope I have words

Through my own loving of a duration without guess

In its spinning space I have without a soil my cords

I belong to the earth again and again as makes toil

With mirror of soul contemplate for a penny-royal

As its crust is webbed in wet, and as place mushed

Stepping along its robes, nor fear of being crushed

The limelight of this morning is as slow to reconcile

To open a mind to its words in its silent elevations

Am I the jongleur through paradise's assignations?

Pavements of this ground, terrains are made tiles

Without losing sight, a passing nights trivialization

Parsing lost in the construct of sleep's imagination

– They are the shrews of a wilderness, me, I am
in its aliveness –

It brings daylight to me

Like casting net it surprises me ungloved

A parade, my own daylight where parallels

Cast their shine on me, as I wait for a sun

A surging through the open sky in flannel

Desire is plain and tired without sinecure

Through seamless night pain hurls muscle

In gormlessness the back a straddled time

Troubled by a causeway of fishing, a line

Over heaps and mounds, makes demand

Constructed, constrained to have a sieve

Driven to its plenitude made from peeve

Overturning in lust has grimes of its sand

Turning wheels for daylights compassion

Walking listless, Diogenes talking fashion

– Coming out of being smothered, stand up straight –

Noel Jeffs

Licker split

In poetry I am made complete
I am made complete in poetry
– In silence I mirror –
– In silence I am formed – worlds,
Are realised
Just a pickle to borrow from its surroundings

I was pushed and pulled and made into licker spit

But I crept through the night and forward was pain

Hovered lightly through its apprehensions said flit

And touched my own garment again in its service

Viewed a strange world, was though it never was

But will be there tomorrow borrowed as its chase

As dawning begins to parade itself through my life

And I trebled less had no clef but was given in rife

Had I tied a gorgons knot or just made into a sieve

Opened a doorway to slight, or was in turning tide

Daylight warming slowly through horizons of light

Ran up its chase like ague had made into a release

And trusted my own ram's horn to make a shawm

Where daylight has increased, encased in warmth

Today's fray

To find my desk like a plate turned to its hour

Without tunnel vision marked day as crimson

Am holding space within passion of its glower

To settle slowly, to making the hay of damson

Beyond glitch and parade, as holding my chest

Watched sunshine's beginning imbroglio vest

Through this holms glen to signal for my own

As though testily, one day is after other sown

Walking streets where neither is more driven

And I capture the grace of birds made in flight

If companionship was true, as it's holding light

To hold in this tribe was a moment of its riven

The river is mine in its country of long guiding

Where stars are not flannel in passages eliding

Noel Jeffs

In morning light as it drizzles for sunshine

A strange coquette that parades daylight

Like a tumbril, as it breaks the day of line

Where quietness has its mirror of a plight

Have I been trampled located in its time?

Seared and not wanting, searching grime

Overhead the openness has its vagrancy

The sky is waiting in a coldness, clemency

Timorous as for the first rays of a trailing

Light as it begins a day of this enhancing

There is little sand made for its prancing

Windswept in its lightness makes gulling

Seasoned for a dryness as a nevertheless

Opening spaces are mine for cravenness

Unfazed

Refuse to be disavowed some are disenfranchised but exercise their
power, refuse to be dispossessed

It is a cold morning of its own haze

My lips are vented beyond surprise

My clenched teeth a grit their faze

Holding the words to begin silence

Thinking of the graze in its clocked

Consuming the space for as kicked

Beyond harrowing has word poetic

And like a snake pursuing as phrase

Nothing a dilemma tastes diamante

As a path laden in rivers frow mine

Like gammon searches stayed time

Through streets of whorls a Levant

Laden whirlpools crave as whirligigs

In the opening doors breathing figs

Noel Jeffs

In the beam of this first daylight's spray

Touching its cordon of light as it glows

Searing has an openness or a skies lay

Touching venue of today's time flows

Loudly it proclaims in its early silence

Touches my fences as through license

Out of this looming of its gaming voice

Moves through like a gliding of a train

Slowly as though not spent in a river's

Catching its coasting of its own image

Where coastlines sails a raft's tonnage

Touching seemingly spent dawns cliffs

Here a limpid lake made of a drawing

Where spokes of noise cry awakening

It is a morning light not diminished by its sky

It is a realm of slow awakening, long violence

But sunlight is light but streaming has its kite

Where guessing I am opening a door's insight

Through all its labels quests and income slight

It is my wandering through sanity of my mind

Not grim, but crikey open eyes to angers kiln

Where it whistles for a wind, mints has clown

Partook of its own perfume and sought as rile

Through daylights timely questioning for grist

Ladles words aspirations again without hissed

Cuddles in time for the owning of a signs guile

Drummed like a beat to open mind as a speak

Saw containing verves that made list to greet

– Tracts for the times –

Noel Jeffs

In morning light I began again today beyond its pain

To venture myself through into a sloping for its day

In a time's vented, as my arm has touched in a rain

Where spaces have opened again into its brave fey

Like a tidal mystery it caters for its drams of a game

Through the cloudlessness has openness sky's cram

Touching its edges with the sedges of its own flame

Wandering though minstrel's crepe as makes claim

Sundered in pity but taken making has as a shadow

Casting through meantime's where it will have face

Like a gaping waiting to be filled, as its strides a race

Beyond tranche of rest or pinnacle made of its ladle

The gopher's lips are eating the air, its own vibrancy

Trusting each bubble it becomes a window's gantry

It is a morning caught in its own greyness

A day beckoning through tiredness's eyes

And I refuse nays and says though likeness

Could be made into an eternal pit for tays

I refuse to walk beyond the list of my toes

To catch cold or wet and languish for floes

25

It must rest in the whistle down of its rain

To catch the crispness of this day as a pain

Lust or shine driven or design to rest a like

The eternal languishing as of my own lain

But this is a tempest strung for grey drains

To touch pain or solitude to sleep for dyke

That sees beyond a window consequence

That says sleep is mine, turning sequences

In morning light it shines a daylight of readiness but waiting

Touches the corners of my heart says as time has in heaven

Things may come and go and may be finished it covers fetes

Time is of the essence but in its silence plays hard for leaven

And I open my ears to just a plaid time of my words of saying

Just as the jaw is sore again and requires that play weighing

So I in insist to sit stillness in the rest for its own prioception

Touch the corners of my heart again for slowness as receipt

While the skies lightness of this morning sky wiles for its day

I touch my ears to know they are real allowing space to walk

So that I can gather my own clamour to its face of as talked

What measures its ownership made of play and knows a lay

Triste, sadness, just overwhelmed to crave lying down again

And tints a day in its tint of daylights beginning as like a rain

The morning light is gilding in its spring's turning

Days will become warmer bring heat to a room

This view of railway lines will bring as a looming

Where trains slide past passengers of costume

The open sky sits firmly above like all a heaven

To touch meadows and graze grounds a leaven

Begging for more as turning days into a shining

Clings like surprise as dawning clutters a lining

Touchstone to a rose, a cyclamen sits in verge

And holding the spate of its own rising in pate

A little world a hatter trading moment as gate

Rolling through this ledge a glassy-eyed hedge

Begins day in blooming space has its diamond

Mien of wider world and just as for humankind

– Father's day – can we find a verandah of plain sailing?

The morning light is as fleche across my window

It touches lightly the glass as though it summons

Enduring passing a phase of night and a meadow

Do I taste cinnamon in coffee or its bone heads?

There is pluck in the miles of a sunlight and sign

To touch my own welshing again to taste inside

Heaving a stomach and a hoping for as gamelan

To open my heart for my own glamour is again

Passing all this hectoring of insight and walking

A strange song to say beyond need I talk myself

To gush my bowels beyond a made demonizing

Counterpoint tower's hemstitched line's a craic

Sign of its times whistling to the wind of a barrel

Trusting that if I sit plush or rush, it airs a Farrell

In an early morning light an awakening to trust of life

It is body banking on its desiring of lyrics and lyre-ing

With an even spread of soul into a watchfulness' sief

The upholding of old times and its spreading retrying

Through the stillness of the morning for 1t bakes day

Only the glow of day in sight and I have stood in lay

To hold the face of the mirror again all as made signs

Furnish hope in the standing up again was of its fires

Where the sky is a bald eye as crown of its sown iris

As it begins to evoke its might as made for its insects

And bites through an awakening of its dusts as flecks

Has no quark or meaning other than beyond an egros

As the day open its mind gloaming trial for as veneer

To pander through an occupancy of as seems a queer

– Always my own consecration –

Becoming linear

A syllogism of life they say in a play of its words

Under a blank stage sky touching my own piety

As it is rostrum to its own playfulness a grounds

Touching a muteness as yet of their days gaiety

Although rush and bother as transport will come

To make the spaces of creating its dray marking

As it resembles a maypole its stitch in times resin

To find the kino bleach and ointment holding soil

Circumstances can appear slowly in a substratum

Holiness is not a placard but a mien of gathering

Playing through a singing of open airs lathering

Crumbs the coffee is cooking a laterite of datum

Crotches burn and toil to grounds of their built

Spinning this top into a world of may be as lilts

In the early morning driven sundered until awakening to its dawning

Picked up the pieces that are necessary to make countenance's refuse

Just keeping slippers at the foot of my bed as birds come in a lawning

Do lions speak I do in my own time creep to my owning and partake the

Days may seem slow but the crunch is my own desire and not pathogen

Into this morning light I find words make a prayer beyond being an exile

As the cheapening bird song that manufactured its own loss passed by

And I trust in the blue heavens of today as through boldness was sung

I watch its rumbling through my own dreaming of pages touched in ink

Leisurely and open to my own a parterre of lusting for its own renewal

And a finesse for croissant times in a payment in croyant of the solair

This is not moonshine but my dance for its wandering deserts of myrrh

No need to hurry as it will be all there in the good times of all my days

As it balances life and solitude and find words those as burn for its rays

It is light where it touches day and the renewal of membrane in mind

Passages of time reveal in the moment that is making in its own event

Writing from within is a sword a space within the holding grace of limb

And I am seasoned by duration that daylight's holding a word of a scent

I pause to catch my breath again as it brings my own consuming to hold

A bream full in words and a gathering of each days making has of a fold

It wraps like an implore to upset old stories and make many more mirth

To take sprite as its own in the world shake of Cyrus, a temple in a land

Crying to domain and a resurrection through a canopy of training more

A tor is as mountain's shape and gateway for cow where others prevail

I count all the chips already on my plate and reach to plait in more sand

Can I have cake and eat where I walk thoughts dreaming in the possible

This day of contemplation is whistled vanity of wanting more of a tune

Through nights of rain glistening on container's breezes

Through opening of a day break was all spring unleashes

Through a disseminating knowledge of its own squeezes

Touching my raiment has a coolness after its warm night

As though clay pots make sum of stay as their own story

And reefers were once those cigarettes of apprehension

And I lust somewhere in my own veins of their desiring

As I declaim one page or another in forming it's as voice

Simple or similar elegant of form on this shore of again

Gathering my spats as thought might be worn in a dress

To lash as own viscosity holding wit against deprivation

Trusting through play of words as changes –scape seines

Touching my own solace in a country of queer and light

Touching my own substance of aliveness beyond claim

Acknowledgements

I am indebted to Simeon Kronenberg for encouraging me to bring this to publication as I would have let it die.

I thank Norm Neill for having an early oversight of my composition and corrected me as to say, 'After Pushkin'.

I am blessed by membership in the Society of Saint Francis and all its provinces, for their kindness and guidance has directed me to this opportunity.

I am extremely grateful for the guiding hand of Mark O'Donnell of Digital Colours for bringing the structure of the book together and collated it in a more meaningful way and handing it over to me as it might have got lost in the pandemic and during my time in hospital.

It would not have been possible to bring this thesis to fruition if I had not had the wise hand of Associate professor Kate Lilley of Sydney University and Dr Peter Minter of the same and Judith Beveridge poet and Thor Blomfield now team leader at Saint Vincent De Paul Society Woolloomooloo.

I also remember those who have treated me graciously well and respectfully, wherein I, am now in a world of poetry which is now my inspiration for writing. My mother encouraged me to write.

As spoken, I have since created my world of writing through a master's degree of Creative Writing at Sydney University, and especially I register my thanks to Associate-Professor Kate Lilley. She understood my mind and its processes, and the Disability

Department of Sydney University who gave me their utmost support and helped me gain the degree.

I give thanks for Thor Blomfield and Matthew Egan always at my side in these latter days and giving time and friendship to consolidate this experience.

You will see my friends in this endeavour in their testimonials, and I am grateful that Martin Langford will launch my book and am grateful that IndieMosh and everybody gave me this opportunity to bring it to the world

About the Author

Noel Jeffs SSF is an Anglican Friar originally from Gippsland, Australia. He is a sometimes student of Kate Lilley and others for a Master of Creative Writing at Sydney University. He is a disabled person living alone who enjoys conversations and silence and writing. Noel has a master's degree in Mental Health and has trained as a psychotherapist.

His poetry print publication Under the Dome is still available from Garden Lounge in Newton, Sydney. He has been published in Burrows twice and is currently part of two anthologies, David Reuters' Outer Space/Inner Minds and Antologie Romana Australiana, a cross-cultural work of dialogue and discourse between his Sydney workshop and the 'Palatul Culturii Bistrita-Romania' where he was translated into Romanian.

Notes

In "The Awakened Heart" of Obeyeskere
'The awakened ones, A phenomenology of Visionary experience'

There is a chapter in Book One. Page 45
The visionary experience: theoretical understandings
'Daybreak: the space of silence and the emergence of aphoristic
thinking' …

Columbia University Press 2012.

www.ingramcontent.com/pod-product-compliance
Lightning Source LLC
Chambersburg PA
CBHW051817050726
47598CB00006B/2599